# Soft Skills Sleuths

# CRITICAL THINKING

## INVESTIGATING LIFE SKILLS SUCCESS

Diane Lindsey Reeves with Connie Hansen

Illustrations by Ruth Bennett

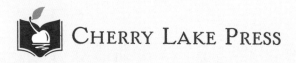

Published in the United States of America by Cherry Lake Publishing Group
Ann Arbor, Michigan
www.cherrylakepublishing.com

Created and produced by Bright Futures Press
www.brightfuturespress.com

Reading Advisor: Marla Conn, MS, Ed., Literacy specialist, Read-Ability, Inc.
Illustrator: Ruth Bennett
Cover and Page Designer: Kathy Heming
Design Elements: © mijatmijatovic/Shutterstock.com; © GoodStudio/Shutterstock.com;
    © Denis Cristo/Shutterstock.com; © Lorelyn Medina/Shutterstock.com; © Yaroshenko Olena/
    Shutterstock.com; © rangsan paidaen/Shutterstock.com

**Cherry Lake Press** is an imprint of Cherry Lake Publishing Group.

Library of Congress Cataloging-in-Publication Data has been filed and is available at catalog.loc.gov

Cherry Lake Publishing Group would like to acknowledge the work of the Partnership for 21st Century
Learning, a Network of Battelle for Kids. Please visit http://www.battelleforkids.org/networks/p21
for more information.

Printed in the United States of America
Corporate Graphics

# TABLE OF CONTENTS

# What Are Soft Skills and

**Skills** are needed to succeed at any job you can imagine. Different jobs require different skills. Professional baseball players need good batting and catching skills. Brain surgeons need steady hands and lots of practice with a scalpel. These are examples of **hard skills** necessary to do specific jobs.

Everyone needs "**soft skills**" to succeed in life. Soft skills get personal. They are about how you behave and treat people. Soft skills are the skills you need to be the very best *you* at home, work, and school.

"Sounds good," you say. "But I don't have a job. Why do I need to worry about soft skills?"

Ahh, but you do have a job. In fact, you have a very important job. You are a student, and your job is to learn as much as you can. Learning soft skills makes you a better student now. It also gets you ready to succeed in any career you choose later.

**Critical Thinking** is the ability to use information to make smart decisions. It is knowing how to think clearly and reasonably. Critical thinking allows you to make logical connections between ideas. It involves thinking on purpose to make sense of different types of situations and challenges.

In this book, you get to be a soft skills sleuth. You will track down clues about what good (and not so good!) critical thinking looks like. You will investigate four critical thinking soft skills cases that include:

- **Problem Solving**
- **Creativity**
- **Self-Regulation**
- **Decision Making**

# Why Do I Need Them?

## HOW TO USE THIS BOOK

Here's how you can be a soft skills sleuth. In each chapter:

 **Gather the facts.** Read the description about the soft skill.

 **Read the case file.** Check out a situation where soft skills are needed.

 **Investigate the case.** Look for clues showing soft skills *successes* and soft skills *mistakes*. Keep track of the clues on a blank sheet of paper.

 **Crack the case.** Did you spot all the clues?

# SOFT SKILL #1

You forget your lunch money at home. Someone makes fun of your new shoes. You don't understand how to do your math homework. These are all examples of the kinds of problems that students like you face every day.

What can you do about problems like these? Well ... you could ignore them and hope they go away. But that means you will go hungry for lunch. You will feel upset all day about being teased. And you will get a bad grade on your math assignment.

Or you could figure out ways to solve the problems. There is usually more than one solution for every problem. You just have to find them. Finding solutions means facing the problem and thinking of ways to turn a bad situation into a good one. Sometimes it means asking for help. For instance, you could ask your teacher for help with the lunch money problem. When someone teases you, you could speak up for yourself and let them know it is not okay. You could ask a friend who is really good at math for help with your homework.

As you get older, your problems will get more **complicated**. That's why learning good **problem-solving** skills now is such a good idea! Get creative with ideas. Ask questions to figure out answers. Share your worry with someone who can help. These are ways to tackle problems big and small.

## Problem-Solving
### Tips

- Say what the problem really is.
- Brainstorm ways to solve the problem.
- List the pros and cons of each solution.
- Make sure everyone agrees on the solution.
- Pick a solution and give it a try.
- If all else fails, try again with Plan B.

"In the middle of difficulty lies opportunity."
—Albert Einstein

# PROBLEM SOLVING

## SOFT SKILLS CASE #1: PROBLEM SOLVING

Ms. Hollis has a brilliant idea for teaching her class about problem solving. She's going to lock them up in a room and tell them to figure out how to get out.

What?!?

No, it's not child abuse. It's a new escape room game at the community center. It's like solving a giant puzzle. Players have to brainstorm ideas and look for ways to get out of the room.

It's time for a field trip! Last one out is a rotten egg!

**DO:**
Investigate
problem solving
successes and
mistakes!

**DO NOT:**
Write in this
book!

SOFT SKILLS SLEUTHS: Investigating Life Skills Success

# HAS ANYONE SEEN THE EXIT?

# PROBLEM SOLVING

Problem-solvers at work here. It's time to come up with an exit plan!

**Start here!**

**Success!**
Working together to come up with ideas.

**Mistake.**
"We're doomed! We're doomed! And I'm freaking out!"

**Success!**
Making a list of possible solutions.

**Mistake.**
Trying to force a solution that just doesn't work.

Did you **find** all the successes and **MISTAKES**?

# How can you turn your challenges into opportunities?

**Mistake.** Worrying your head off.

**Mistake.** Is arguing about it going to help?

**Did you find them all?**

**Success!** Talking about the good and bad points of each solution.

**Mistake.** Maybe if we ignore the problem, it will just go away.

**Success!** Mapping out the options to help find the answer.

**Success!** Trying out ideas to see if they work.

# SOFT SKILL #2

**Creativity** isn't just for artists, musicians, and actors. Their work is certainly creative, and we enjoy the results. Yet sometimes we forget that creativity touches every part of our lives. Smartphones, Fitbit watches, robots—all the coolest new technologies started as a creative idea in someone's mind. Creativity also shows up in simple, everyday ways.

One of the first ways that humans experience creativity is through play. Can you remember playing dress-up or cops and robbers when you were little? If you were like most kids, your **imagination** ran wild! You probably thought you really were a princess, detective, or dinosaur.

Now that you are older, you have to work a little harder to be creative. Experts say that creativity is one of the toughest thinking skills to learn. But, like any other skill, it can be learned with practice. Start some creative habits—write, sing, dance, act, make videos with your phone, create cartoons about funny things you notice, or make up jokes. All of these are ways to flex your creative muscles. Then you will be ready when it comes time to "**think outside the box**" to find ideas for a school project, solutions to a problem, or new ways to do things.

## Thinking Outside the Box

- Ask **what-if** questions to test how well your ideas might work.
- Daydream a little to give your brain a break and then get back to work.
- Exercise to get your heart pumping and improve your mood and add brain power.
- Do your thinking outside on a sunny day to let the blue skies and Mother Nature inspire you.

"You can't use up creativity. The more you use, the more you have."
—Maya Angelou

# CREATIVITY

## SOFT SKILLS CASE #2: CREATIVITY

Mr. Evan is big on recycling. There is nothing he dislikes more than seeing something go to waste. When the recycling bin in his class started to overflow, he decided it was time to put his students' imaginations to work.

The assignment: Turn all that trash into treasures! He wants to see what kind of creative ideas his students can come up with for reusing their trash.

Turn the page to see how well this creative workout is working out!

**DO:**
Investigate creativity successes and mistakes!

**DO NOT:**
Write in this book!

# WHO'S GOT A BRIGHT IDEA?

# CREATIVITY

Are these students doing a good job of turning trash into treasures?

Did you **find** all the *successes* and **MISTAKES**?

**Start here!**

**Success!**
Picturing ideas in your mind before you try them.

**Mistake.**
It's hard to find a good idea in a big mess.

**Mistake.**
Stressing out stops the creative flow in its tracks.

**Success!**
Trying different ways to use your ideas.

**Success!**
Brainstorming with a friend.

CASE NOTES

**What does creativity look like in your world?**

**Mistake.**
Trashing it instead of recycling it.

**Did you find them all?**

**Success!**
Getting creative and one idea adds to another.

**Mistake.**
Giving ideas a chance to work before throwing them out.

**Success!**
Two heads can be better than one. Teamwork!

# SOFT SKILL #3

Sure, you know how to behave yourself when your parents or teachers are watching. The big question is: Do you know how to behave yourself when no one is looking? **Self-regulation** is the ability to control your own behavior.

Self-regulation might mean saying "yes" to something you need to do but might not really want to do. Finishing up your homework without being told is one example. Brushing your teeth and being nice to your siblings are others.

Self-regulation can also mean saying "no" to something you really want to do but shouldn't. This could be as simple as not grabbing cookies out of the pantry before dinner or not talking back to the coach.

Self-regulation is a two-step process. It involves stopping to think and making a choice. First, you need to think about the results of an action. Like the famous scientist Sir Isaac Newton said, "For every action there is a reaction." He was talking about physics. But the same could be said for behavior. Good behavior brings good results. Bad behavior brings trouble.

The ability to control your behavior is a sign of **maturity**. You no longer need constant supervision like little kids do. You gain more freedoms and have the opportunity to keep building your self-regulation skills.

The ability to make good choices is a big step toward adulthood. Plus, it is nice not always being told what to do.

## Ways to Keep **Yourself** Out of **Trouble**

- Follow instructions.
- Think before you act.
- Set clear goals and go after them.
- Stay away from situations (and people) that are likely to get you in trouble.

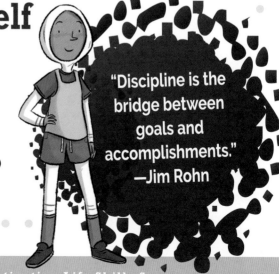

"Discipline is the bridge between goals and accomplishments."
—Jim Rohn

# SELF-REGULATION

## SOFT SKILLS CASE #3: SELF-REGULATION

Mr. Reid has to take an emergency phone call down in the office. He will be right back. In the meantime, he told his class to work quietly on their assignment. He is counting on his students to do the right thing. That way, no one gets hurt or in trouble.

These directions are proving to be easier for some students to follow than for others. Which students show signs of self-regulation in the classroom pictured on the next page?

**DO:** Investigate self-regulation successes and mistakes!

**DO NOT:** Write in this book!

# WHO HAS THEIR ACT TOGETHER?

# SELF-REGULATION

The proof is in the behavior. Are these students self-regulated or not?

Did you **find** all the successes and **MISTAKES**?

## Start here!

## Success!
Self-regulation is happening everywhere!

## Mistake.
Yoo-hoo! Did you lose your seat?

## Mistake.
Stop pestering the class pet.

# CASE NOTES

## How are your self-regulation skills behaving?

**Success!** Helping out a classmate.

**Mistake.** Shooting spit wads? Really?

**Did you find them all?**

**Mistake.** Scribbling on the board isn't a good look.

**Success!** Self-discipline now, no homework later.

**Mistake.** How about minding your own business?

# SOFT SKILL #4

You make lots of decisions every day. Do you want a hamburger or pizza for lunch? A blue backpack or a red one? Would you rather sign up for the soccer team or the STEM club? Some decisions are easy. They are important at the time, but you could go either way without messing up your life.

Some decisions are huge. They can mean the difference between a happy, fulfilled life and a lot of regret. When you are an adult, you will eventually face big life-changing decisions. What career do you want to pursue? Who do you want to choose as a life partner? Where do you want to live?

How do you get ready to make those big decisions? By learning how to handle little decisions right now. The first thing to keep in mind is that **decision making** is a thinking skill. Sure, your emotions play a role (you are human, after all), but you can't let emotions run the show! Think about what you really want. Think about what will happen if you say yes. Think about what will happen if you say no. Think about whether or not you would be happy with the same decision tomorrow, next month, or even years down the road.

Little decisions sometimes boil down to "eenie, meenie, miney, mo." Just make a choice and move on. Big decisions are better when you think them through.

## Keys to Making Good Decisions

- Gather the facts.
- Ask yourself **what-if** questions.
- Ask for advice.
- Give yourself time to think things through.
- Don't sweat the small stuff.

"Simple it's not,
I am afraid you
will find, for a
mind-maker-upper
to make up his mind."
—Dr. Seuss

# DECISION MAKING

## SOFT SKILLS CASE #4: DECISION MAKING

Mr. Conrad's backpacking club is preparing for a hiking trip into a national park where they will sleep under the stars! The only thing around them will be the great outdoors. There will be no drive-through restaurants. No hotels to sleep in. No hot showers to freshen up in.

Their challenge is to pack everything they will need to be comfortable (and survive!) for the overnight adventure. Since they have to carry everything they bring, good decision making will help lighten the load. Look at the scene on the next page. Which wannabe campers are making good decisions?

**DO:**
Investigate decision making successes and mistakes!

**DO NOT:**
Write in this book!

Camping trips are more fun when you make good decisions about what to bring.

READY OR NOT.
HERE THEY COME!

# DECISION MAKING

Are these students ready for a great outdoor adventure? Which ones are making good decisions about what to bring?

Did you **find** all the successes and **MISTAKES**?

**Start here!**

**Success!**
Making a list and checking it twice.

**Mistake.**
Stop thinking and decide already!

**Mistake.**
Is it really that important to get your own way about everything?

# Have you decided to make good decisions?

**Success!**
Helping each other make a good plan.

**Success!**
Teamwork!

**Did you find them all?**

**Success!**
Weather watchers know what kind of socks to pack.

**Mistake.**
Packing too much of a good thing.

**Success!**
Everyone gets a say!

# WHAT HAVE YOU Learned?

# CRITICAL THINKING ······▸ Q U I Z

**Question 1:**

Critical thinking helps you make
_____
decisions.

**Question 2:**

One way to solve a problem is to ask for _____.

**Question 3:**

_____ problems won't make them go away.

**Question 4:**

One of the hardest critical-thinking skills to learn is
_____.

**Question 5:**

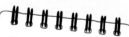 is one of the first ways humans experience creativity.

**Question 6:**

Self-regulation is the ability to
_____
your own behavior.

**Question 7:**

Self-regulation means you _____ to do the right thing.

**Question 8:**

Decision making is a _____ skill.

Critical thinking soft skills start here!

# GLOSSARY

**complicated** (KAHM-plih-kate-id) made difficult because of the many different parts or ideas

**creativity** (kree-ay-TIV-ih-tee) skillful at using imagination and thinking up new ideas

**decision making** (dih-SIZH-uhn MAKE-ing) the process of making a choice or drawing a conclusion about something

**hard skills** (HAHRD SKILZ) specific skills needed to do a specific job

**imagination** (ih-maj-uh-NAY-shuhn) the ability to form pictures in your mind of things that are not present or real

**investigate** (in-VES-tih-gate) to gather information or clues about something

**maturity** (muh-CHOOR-ih-tee) the quality of behaving mentally and emotionally like an adult

**problem solving** (PRAH-bluhm SAHLV-ing) the process of working through a difficult situation or making hard decisions

**second-guessing** (SEK-uhnd GES-ing) questioning your opinions or actions about a decision that has already been made

**self-regulation** (SELF reg-yuh-LAY-shuhn) the ability to control one's own behavior

**sleuth** (SLOOTH) a detective or person who is good at finding facts and clues

**soft skills** (SAWFT SKILZ) behaviors and personality traits people use every day to succeed in life

**think outside the box** (THINGK out-SIDE THUH BAHKS) think in an original or creative way

**what-if** (WAHT IF) a question that supposes something

# INDEX

# ABOUT THE AUTHORS

**Diane Lindsey Reeves** likes to write books that help students figure out what they want to be when they grow up. She mostly lives in Washington, D.C., but spends as much time as she can in North Carolina and South Carolina with her grandkids.

**Connie Hansen** spent 25 years teaching college students about successful life skills. She lives in Lynchburg, Virginia where her favorite thing to do is play with her grandchildren. Her happy place is the beach!

# ABOUT THE ILLUSTRATOR

**Ruth Bennett** lives in a small country village in the heart of Norfolk, England, with her two cats, Queen Elizabeth and Queen Victoria. She loves petting dogs, watching movies, and drawing, of course!